A Note From Rick Renner

I am on a personal quest to see a "revival of the Bible" so people can establish their lives on a firm foundation that will stand strong and endure the test when the end-time storm winds begin to intensify.

In order to experience a revival of the Bible in your personal life, it is important to take time each day to read, receive, and apply its truths to your life. James tells us that if we will continue in the perfect law of liberty — refusing to be forgetful hearers but determined to be doers — we will be blessed in our ways. As you watch or listen to the programs in this series and work through this corresponding study guide, I trust that you will search the Scriptures and allow the Holy Spirit to help you hear something new from God's Word that applies specifically to your life. I encourage you to be a doer of the Word that He reveals to you. Whatever the cost, I assure you — it will be worth it.

> Thy words were found, and I did eat them;
> and thy word was unto me the joy and rejoicing of mine heart:
> for I am called by thy name, O Lord God of hosts.
> — Jeremiah 15:16

Your brother and friend in Jesus Christ,

Rick Renner

Rick Renner

Being in the Right Place at the Right Time

Copyright © 2020 by Rick Renner
8316 E. 73rd St.
Tulsa, Oklahoma 74133

Published by Rick Renner Ministries
www.renner.org

ISBN 13: 978-1-68031-804-3

eBook ISBN 13: 978-1-68031-805-0

How To Use This Study Guide

This five-lesson study guide corresponds to *"Being in the Right Place at the Right Time" With Rick Renner* (Renner TV). Each lesson in this study guide covers a topic that is addressed during the program series, with questions and references supplied to draw you deeper into your own private study of the Scriptures on this subject.

To derive the most benefit from this study guide, consider the following:

First, watch or listen to the program prior to working through the corresponding lesson in this guide. (Programs can also be viewed at **renner.org** by clicking on the Media/Archives links.)

Second, take the time to look up the scriptures included in each lesson. Prayerfully consider their application to your own life.

Third, use a journal or notebook to make note of your answers to each lesson's Study Questions and Practical Application challenges.

Fourth, invest specific time in prayer and in the Word of God to consult with the Holy Spirit. Write down the scriptures or insights He reveals to you.

Finally, take action! Whatever the Lord tells you to do according to His Word, do it.

For added insights on this subject, it is recommended that you obtain Rick Renner's book *The Will of God: The Key to Your Success*. You may also select from Rick's other available resources by placing your order at **renner.org** or by calling 1-800-742-5593.

TOPIC

The Church at Antioch

SCRIPTURES

1. **Acts 13:1** — Now there were in the church that was at Antioch certain prophets and teachers; as Barnabas, and Simeon that was called Niger, and Lucius of Cyrene, and Manaen, which had been brought up with Herod the tetrarch, and Saul.

2. **Acts 11:19-28** — Now they which were scattered abroad upon the persecution that arose about Stephen travelled as far as Phenice, and Cyprus, and Antioch, preaching the word to none but unto the Jews only. And some of them were men of Cyprus and Cyrene, which, when they were come to Antioch, spake unto the Grecians, preaching the Lord Jesus. And the hand of the Lord was with them: and a great number believed, and turned unto the Lord. Then tidings of these things came unto the ears of the church which was in Jerusalem: and they sent forth Barnabas, that he should go as far as Antioch. Who, when he came, and had seen the grace of God, was glad, and exhorted them all, that with purpose of heart they would cleave unto the Lord. For he was a good man, and full of the Holy Ghost and of faith: and much people was added unto the Lord. Then departed Barnabas to Tarsus, for to seek Saul. And when he had found him, he brought him unto Antioch. And it came to pass, that a whole year they assembled themselves with the church, and taught much people. And the disciples were called Christians first in Antioch. And in these days came prophets from Jerusalem unto Antioch. And there stood up one of them named Agabus, and signified by the Spirit that there should be a dearth throughout all the world: which came to pass during the days of Claudius Caesar.

GREEK WORDS

1. "there were" — ἦσαν (*esan*): there existed
2. "now" — δὲ (*de*): an exclamatory statement
3. "in" — κατά (*kata*): carries the sense of domination

4. "church" — ἐκκλησία (*ekklesia*): a called, separated, and prestigious assembly; used to denote a prestigious assembly of distinguished Athenian citizens who determined laws, debated public policy, formulated new policies, argued and ruled in judicial matters, elected the chief magistrates of the land, decided who should be banished; to be selected from society and invited to join this assembly was a great honor; in the New Testament, it depicts the body of believers who have been called out, called forth, selected, and assembled to be God's representatives in every town, city, state or nation; a body called to make decisions that affects the atmosphere of a region

5. "certain" — οὖσαν (*ousan*): a form of εἰμί (*eimi*); here, existing; having life and flourishing

6. "prophets" — προφήτης (*prophetes*): a compound of the words πρό (*pro*) and φημί (*phemi*); the word πρό (*pro*) is used in connection with *phemi*, which always means to say or to speak

7. "teachers" — διδάσκαλος (*didaskalos*): here, plural; teachers; one who is a fabulous, masterful teacher; the Greek equivalent for the Hebrew word rabbi

SYNOPSIS

The five lessons in this study, *Being in the Right Place at the Right Time*, will focus on the following topics:

- The Church at Antioch
- The Unique Mix of Leadership in Antioch
- The Right Place at the Right Time
- The Right Balance for a Powerful Environment
- Are You in the Right Place for God To Develop You?

The emphasis of this lesson:

Antioch was a magnificent, thriving city located about 445 miles north of Jerusalem. It was founded in the fourth century BC and became the home of a powerful church during the First Century. The pivotal role it played in the emergence of early Christianity caused Antioch to become known as "the cradle of Christianity."

The book of Acts records that there was a thriving church in the city of Antioch that was birthed during the First Century. What you may not know is that the first meeting place of this congregation was a cave. This cave was located in the center of a *necropolis*, which in Greek literally means *city of the dead*. That's right — the church of Antioch was located in a graveyard!

Why would church members meet in a graveyard? The reason is clear: no one bothered them there. The pagans left them alone. The necropolis where the church of Antioch met was dedicated to Charon, the god of the underworld. It was believed that Charon transported departed souls from the land of the living across the River Styx into hades. Thus, the place where the church of Antioch met was a very dark burial site that the pagans avoided.

Isn't it interesting that in this dreary, dismal environment the Christian Church actually thrived. It confirms God's Word in Romans 5:20, which says, "...Where sin abounded, grace did much more abound." Indeed, the church was flourishing in Antioch. It was there that a man named Saul — who would later become known as the apostle Paul — was trained to be a preacher and teacher to the Gentiles. It proved to be the right place and the right time for him to be there.

The Bible's First Description of the Church of Antioch

The church at Antioch was an important part of the work God was doing in the Early Church. In Acts 13:1, the historian Luke wrote, "Now there were in the church that was at Antioch certain prophets and teachers; as Barnabas, and Simeon that was called Niger, and Lucius of Cyrene, and Manaen, which had been brought up with Herod the tetrarch, and Saul."

This verse opens with the word "now," which is the Greek word *de*, and it is used here as *an exclamatory statement*. It is almost as if the Holy Spirit is lifting His voice saying, "Wow! What was taking place in the city of Antioch was absolutely amazing."

The verse goes on to say, "...There were in the church...." The words "there were" are also significant. It is the Greek word *esan*, which would better be translated *there existed*. Even the two-letter word "in" is important. It is the Greek word *kata*, which always carries the idea of *domination*. Thus, Luke wrote, "Wow! What existed in and dominated the church at Antioch was incredible!"

This brings us to the word "church," which is the Greek word *ekklesia*, the same word translated as "church" all throughout the New Testament. It is a compound of the word *ek*, meaning *out*, and a form of the word *kaleo*, which means *to call or beckon*. When these two words are joined to form the new word *ekklesia*, it describes *a called, separated, and prestigious assembly*.

What is interesting is that this word didn't originate in the church world. It was borrowed from Athenian culture and was used to denote *a prestigious assembly of distinguished Athenian citizens who determined laws, debated public policy, formulated new policies, argued and ruled in judicial matters, elected the chief magistrates of the land, and decided who should be banished*. To be selected from society and invited to join this assembly was a great honor.

The writers of the New Testament fully understood this meaning, and they selected the word *ekklesia* to depict *the body of believers who have been called out, called forth, selected, and assembled to be God's representatives in every town, city, state or nation*. The Church is not a club that meets in various buildings around the world. The Church is *a body called to make decisions that affects the atmosphere of a region*.

The History of Antioch

The ancient Greek city of Antioch was located on the eastern side of the Orontes River. Its ruins lie within the confines of the modern city of Antakya, Turkey. Antioch was founded near the end of the fourth century BC by one of Alexander the Great's generals, which made it a very prestigious city. The city's geographic location made it very important militarily, and its economic power caused it to be one of the most powerful cities in the Roman Empire. In fact, it was one of the seven largest cities in the entire Roman Empire. It's location benefited its occupants, with such features as the spice trade, the Silk Road, and the Royal Road. Eventually, Antioch rivaled Alexandria as the chief city of the Near East.

Furthermore, Antioch became one of the most important cities in the eastern Mediterranean of Rome's dominions. At one point during the time of Augustus, it is understood that the city had up to 250,000 people, which was a massive city in the Roman world. Roman emperors saw Antioch as a more suitable capital for the eastern part of the empire than

Alexandria because of Alexandria's isolated position in northern Egypt. Antioch was centrally located to nearly everything.

Even the distinguished Julius Caesar visited the city in 47 BC. Later, both Agrippa and Tiberius enlarged the theatre there, but because they weren't able to finish the work, Emperor Trajan completed it. Afterwards, Antoninus Pius paved the central street of Antioch with granite, giving way to the city having its own circus, which was really a racetrack modeled after the Circus Maximus in the city of Rome.

Indeed, the city of Antioch was stunning. It featured beautiful colonnades, a great number of bath houses, and many aqueducts that bore the names of the Roman Caesars who built them — the finest being the work of Emperor Hadrian. Even King Herod left his mark on Antioch, ordering the construction of a long stoa on the east side of the city. Stoas were covered colonnades with exquisite mosaics carved into the underlying pavement. They had huge, hand-carved columns that supported terracotta roofs and walls that were covered with elaborate frescos. Without question, it was hard to find a more spectacular city.

When Emperor Titus ransacked the city of Jerusalem in 70 AD, he took the cherubim that formally sat atop the Ark of the Covenant in the Holy of Holies and he placed them on top of one of the gates that led into the city of Antioch. These facts are a sampling of what we know about this legendary city, and because of its longevity and the pivotal role that it played in the emergence of early Christianity, Antioch became known as "the cradle of Christianity."

Early Church Activities in Antioch

Interestingly, the city of Antioch had a large Jewish population, and that attracted the earliest missionaries. In fact, historical records indicate that the city of Antioch was first evangelized by the apostle Peter himself around the time when believers first began to leave Jerusalem after Stephen was martyred. When Saul of Tarsus launched a citywide persecution against the church in Jerusalem, the believers were scattered everywhere (*see* Acts 8:4). Early history tells us that Peter left Jerusalem and traveled 445 miles (or 750 kilometers) north to Antioch and began to preach to the Jewish population. With a surge of individuals coming to Christ, Peter established the church at Antioch — possibly in the year 37 or 38 AD.

Some of the details of the growth and activities of the church at Antioch can also be found in Acts 11:19-21, which says:

> **Now they which were scattered abroad upon the persecution that arose about Stephen travelled as far as Phenice, and Cyprus, and Antioch, preaching the word to none but unto the Jews only. And some of them were men of Cyprus and Cyrene, which, when they were come to Antioch, spake unto the Grecians, preaching the Lord Jesus. And the hand of the Lord was with them: and a great number believed, and turned unto the Lord.**

Initially, the Gospel was preached only to the Jews. But when men from Cyprus and Cyrene came to Antioch, they preached to the Grecians, which actually refers to the Gentile population. Since the Gentile Pentecost had already taken place at Cornelius' home (*see* Acts 10:44-48), the Church leaders had begun to expand their efforts of sharing the Gospel to include the Gentiles. The story continues in Acts 11:22-24:

> **Then tidings of these things came unto the ears of the church which was in Jerusalem: and they sent forth Barnabas, that he should go as far as Antioch. Who, when he came, and had seen the grace of God, was glad, and exhorted them all, that with purpose of heart they would cleave unto the Lord. For he was a good man, and full of the Holy Ghost and of faith: and much people was added unto the Lord.**

Again and again, we see and hear about the church at Antioch and how the Holy Spirit was working among the people. The receptivity of the Gospel was growing, and the church was flourishing. Jews and Gentiles alike were coming into the Kingdom, and the cradle of Christianity was created.

Acts 6:5 tells us that one of the very first deacons that the apostles picked to serve in the church in Jerusalem was from Antioch. His name was Nicolas and he was "a proselyte of Antioch." We will see in the coming lessons that it was from the church at Antioch that Paul first launched out into his apostolic ministry, but it would not be without the personal involvement of Barnabas — the "son of encouragement."

Barnabas Searched for and Found Paul

Once Barnabas established his ministry in Antioch, the Bible tells us he did something that literally changed the course of Christianity. Scripture says, "Then departed Barnabas to Tarsus, for to seek Saul" (Acts 11:25). The word "seek" here means *to thoroughly investigate and search out*. Barnabas was determined to find Saul — who we know to be Paul — and he would not leave Tarsus until Paul was at his side.

If you remember, after Paul met Christ on the road to Damascus and was saved, he immediately began to preach the Gospel to the Jews in Damascus. When a group of divisive Jews took counsel to kill Paul, some disciples helped him escape, and he came to Jerusalem. Unfortunately, the believers in Jerusalem were afraid of Paul and didn't believe he was truly saved. It was Barnabas who took Paul under his wing and vouched for his character before the apostles.

Regrettably, the same thing that happened in Damascus began happening again in Jerusalem. As Paul began to debate the Gospel, certain people plotted to kill him. When the church leaders in Jerusalem learned of the assassination plot, they took Paul to Caesarea and put him on a boat and sent him back to his homeland of Tarsus.

Clearly, Barnabas never forgot about Paul, and once he reached an opportune time to pull away, he left Antioch to go find Paul. The Bible says, "And when he had found him, he brought him unto Antioch. And it came to pass, that a whole year they assembled themselves with the church, and taught much people. And the disciples were called Christians first in Antioch" (Acts 11:26).

The word "found" in this verse is the Greek word *eurisko*, which pictures *a moment of exhilaration when a discovery is made after a diligent, extensive search*. It is where we get the word *eureka*. Once Barnabas "found" Paul, Scripture says he "brought" him to Antioch. In Greek, the word "brought" is *ago*, which means *to lead*. In that moment, Barnabas became spiritually responsible for Paul and led him to Antioch, not Jerusalem. This was divinely significant, as we will see more clearly in our coming lessons.

It was in Antioch that the followers of Jesus were first called Christians, and it was the pagans who gave them this name. In Greek, the word "Christians" is *Christos*, which means *anointed*; it is where we get the name *Christ*. Hence, Christians are *little anointed ones*, or *little Christs*. In the

First Century, these individuals carried the same anointing of Jesus and were going around doing what He did — healing the sick, casting out demons, performing miracles, and teaching God's Word.

Just think: What would have become of Paul had Barnabas not gone out to search for him? It is possible that we may not have Paul's writings, which make up a large portion of the New Testament. The fact is, we have Paul's powerful revelations and ministry results because Barnabas didn't give up on him. Do you know of people who have come to Christ but have fallen away from fellowship? It may be that God wants to use you to help them return to the faith.

STUDY QUESTIONS

> **Study to shew thyself approved unto God, a workman that needeth not to be ashamed, rightly dividing the word of truth.**
> **— 2 Timothy 2:15**

1. The very first mention of Barnabas in Scripture is in Acts 4:32-36. What does this passage tell you about the character of this disciple of Christ? What did he do and how did his actions help to tangibly advance the Kingdom of God?
2. The ancient city of Antioch was a massive, marvelous metropolis for many centuries after it was founded by one of Alexander the Great's generals. Name three aspects about this city that you learned in this lesson that most intrigued you.

PRACTICAL APPLICATION

> **But be ye doers of the word, and not hearers only, deceiving your own selves.**
> **— James 1:22**

1. Carefully reread the meaning of the Greek word *ekklesia*, the word for "church" in the New Testament. In what ways is this definition of the Church a new and radical perspective for you? In what ways are you personally living up to the purpose of the Church? In what areas do you know you need God's help to come up higher?

2. Do you know of someone who was once serving Christ but has since fallen away from fellowship? If so, who is it? How can you follow Barnabas' example and help this person return to their faith in Jesus?

TOPIC

The Unique Mix of Leadership in Antioch

SCRIPTURES

1. **Acts 13:1** — Now there were in the church that was at Antioch certain prophets and teachers; as Barnabas, and Simeon that was called Niger, and Lucius of Cyrene, and Manaen, which had been brought up with Herod the tetrarch, and Saul.

2. **Acts 11:19-28** — Now they which were scattered abroad upon the persecution that arose about Stephen travelled as far as Phenice, and Cyprus, and Antioch, preaching the word to none but unto the Jews only. And some of them were men of Cyprus and Cyrene, which, when they were come to Antioch, spake unto the Grecians, preaching the Lord Jesus. And the hand of the Lord was with them: and a great number believed, and turned unto the Lord. Then tidings of these things came unto the ears of the church which was in Jerusalem: and they sent forth Barnabas, that he should go as far as Antioch. Who, when he came, and had seen the grace of God, was glad, and exhorted them all, that with purpose of heart they would cleave unto the Lord. For he was a good man, and full of the Holy Ghost and of faith: and much people was added unto the Lord. Then departed Barnabas to Tarsus, for to seek Saul. And when he had found him, he brought him unto Antioch. And it came to pass, that a whole year they assembled themselves with the church, and taught much people. And the disciples were called Christians first in Antioch. And in these days came prophets from Jerusalem unto Antioch. And there stood up one of them named Agabus, and signified by the Spirit that there should be a dearth throughout all the world: which came to pass during the days of Claudius Caesar.

GREEK WORDS

1. "there were" — ἦσαν (*esan*): there existed
2. "now" — δὲ (*de*): an exclamatory statement
3. "in" — κατά (*kata*): carries the sense of domination
4. "certain" — οὖσαν (*ousan*): a form of εἰμί (*eimi*); here, existing; having life and flourishing
5. "prophets" — προφήτης (*prophetes*): a compound of the words πρό (*pro*) and φημί (*phemi*); the word πρό (*pro*) is used in connection with *phemi*, which always means to say or to speak
6. "teachers" — διδάσκαλος (*didaskalos*): here, plural; teachers; one who is a fabulous, masterful teacher; the Greek equivalent for the Hebrew word rabbi

SYNOPSIS

As we noted in our first lesson, the original meeting place of the members of the church of Antioch was a cave located in a cemetery. And it was in Antioch that believers were first called Christians. After the stoning of Stephen, persecution broke out against the church in Jerusalem, and believers were scattered abroad. Some of them came to Antioch, which was about 445 miles (or 750 kilometers) away, and with them came the message of the Gospel.

Initially, the good news of Jesus was shared only with Jews. But as time passed, many Gentiles in Antioch began hearing and responding to the Gospel, creating what we have come to know as "the new man." Just imagine — converted Jews and Gentiles were worshiping the One True God, side by side, in the same place! In a short period of time, the church of Antioch became a cultural melting pot made up of men and women of different nationalities and ethnicities from all parts of the region. God was building His dream for the Church, and He is still building this dream for the Church today.

The emphasis of this lesson:

In the church at Antioch, the fivefold ministry gifts were flourishing — especially the gifts of the prophet and the teacher. A close look at Scripture reveals that Barnabas, Simeon, and Lucius were prophets; Manaen

and Paul were teachers. The gathering together of this culturally diverse group could only have been done by the hand of God.

A Review of Our Anchor Verse

In Acts 13:1, we see that God was creating something truly special in Antioch that had never been created before. The Bible says, "Now there were in the church that was at Antioch certain prophets and teachers; as Barnabas, and Simeon that was called Niger, and Lucius of Cyrene, and Manaen, which had been brought up with Herod the tetrarch, and Saul."

This verse is simply amazing! It opens with the word "now," which is the Greek word *de*, and it is used here as *an exclamatory statement*. It is almost as if the Holy Spirit is lifting His voice and saying, "Wow! What was taking place in the city of Antioch was extraordinary!"

The next two words in this passage — "there were" — is a translation of the Greek word *esan*, which would better be translated *there existed* or *flourishing there*. The implication here is that the fivefold ministry gifts were visibly thriving in Antioch. These gifts are noted in Ephesians 4:11 and include apostles, prophets, evangelists, pastors, and teachers.

Interestingly, even the two-letter word "in" is important. It is the Greek word *kata*, which always carries the idea of *domination*. The use of these words — "Now there were in" — tells us that the fivefold ministry gifts were not only flourishing in the church at Antioch but they were a powerful dominating force. It was this church that became known as the "cradle of Christianity." From here, the Gospel began to be dispersed throughout the entire region of Asia, which today is modern-day Turkey.

Persecution Produced a Positive Paradigm Shift in the Church

A pivotal point in the formation of the Early Church came when Saul of Tarsus issued orders for Stephen to be stoned to death and then began relentlessly persecuting believers in Jerusalem. He was such a scourge to the Church, the Bible says, "Therefore they [the believers] that were scattered abroad went every where preaching the word" (Acts 8:4). Early history says it was at this time that Peter himself left the city of Jerusalem and traveled north to the city of Antioch, where he began to preach the Gospel to the large Jewish community living there. This may have taken place as early as 37 or 38 AD. In fact, if you study the ancient city of Antioch, historians attribute the founding of the church there to Peter.

Time passed, persecution continued, and more Christians were dispersed throughout the region — many making their way to the city of Antioch. This time when they came, they preached not only to Jews, but also to Greeks. At this point, God had already established a new protocol of ministry to the Gentiles by baptizing Cornelius and his entire household in the Holy Spirit. Now everyone in the world were potential recipients of the Good News. The historian Luke records some of what took place in Acts 11:

> **Now they which were scattered abroad upon the persecution that arose about Stephen travelled as far as Phenice, and Cyprus, and Antioch, preaching the word to none but unto the Jews only.**
>
> **And some of them were men of Cyprus and Cyrene, which, when they were come to Antioch, spake unto the Grecians, preaching the Lord Jesus.**
>
> **Acts 11:19,20**

We noted that the word "Grecians" in verse 20 doesn't refer to Greek-speaking Jews; it denotes pagans. This was a major paradigm shift for the formation of the Church. Gentiles were now included in this fresh, unprecedented move of the Spirit of God. Hence, the church at Antioch became a brand-new breed of believers. For the first time Jews and Gentiles were side by side, worshiping God in the same place. The Bible goes on to say:

> **And the hand of the Lord was with them: and a great number believed, and turned unto the Lord.**
>
> **Acts 11:21**

According to this verse, a spiritual awakening was taking place. Large masses of people — including many Gentiles — were coming to Christ and surrendering their lives to His lordship. This was truly revolutionary. The Scripture then adds:

> **Then tidings of these things came unto the ears of the church which was in Jerusalem: and they sent forth Barnabas, that he should go as far as Antioch. Who, when he came, and had seen**

**the grace of God, was glad, and exhorted them all, that with
purpose of heart they would cleave unto the Lord. For he was
a good man, and full of the Holy Ghost and of faith: and much
people was added unto the Lord.**

Acts 11:22-24

The Barnabas-Paul Connection

Although Barnabas isn't talked about as often as some of the other church leaders, he played a very significant role in the founding and development of the Church. Once he had accomplished his purpose for coming to Antioch, the Bible says, "Then departed Barnabas to Tarsus, for to seek Saul" (Acts 11:25).

Saul, who we know became Paul, was radically saved on the road to Damascus, and his methods of evangelism at the onset were radical as well. In fact, he caused such a ruckus in Jerusalem that the church leaders there put him on a boat and sent him back to his home country of Tarsus (*see* Acts 9:30). But Barnabas had a special place in his heart for Paul, and he decided to go to Tarsus and thoroughly search for Paul until he found him.

The truth is, there are Christians who leave the Church for all kinds of reasons, and many are never seen again. They don't understand why certain decisions were made or they are treated poorly by other believers, and they become offended and leave. What would have happened had Barnabas not gone out and looked for Paul? It's very possible that we would not have the New Testament epistles (books) he wrote, nor would we have the influence and shaping he brought to the Church.

Thankfully, Barnabas' search-and-rescue efforts were successful. Acts 11:26 says, "And when he had found him, he brought him unto Antioch. And it came to pass, that a whole year they assembled themselves with the church, and taught much people. And the disciples were called Christians first in Antioch."

The word "found" here is the Greek word *eurisko*, and it depicts *a moment of exhilaration when a discovery is made after a diligent, extensive search*. It is where we get the word *eureka*. When Barnabas "found" Paul, he brought him to Antioch, not Jerusalem, which was clearly a God-directed move. Antioch was the right place for Paul to be, and it was the right time for him to be there. For one year, Barnabas and Paul remained at the church in Antioch, connecting with the members and teaching them the Word of God.

The Office of a 'Prophet'

Turning our focus once more to Acts 13:1, it says, "Now there were in the church that was at Antioch certain prophets and teachers; as Barnabas, and Simeon that was called Niger, and Lucius of Cyrene, and Manaen, which had been brought up with Herod the tetrarch, and Saul."

Notice the words "certain prophets." In Greek, the word "certain" is *ousan*, which is a form of the word *eimi*, and here, it describes *something existing* or *having life and flourishing*. Again, this indicates that the fivefold ministry gifts were thriving in Antioch — especially the gifts of the prophet and teacher.

The word "prophets" is a form of the Greek word *prophetes*, which is a compound of the words *pro* and *phemi*. The word *pro* is used in connection with *phemi*, which always means *to say or to speak*, and the word *pro* carries four specific ideas: *before*, *in front of*, *on behalf of*, and *in advance*. These are the four aspects of a prophet's ministry.

1. **Prophets speak before the Lord**

   The Greek word *pro* can describe a prophet's position *before God*. The primary ministry of a prophet is to be fellowshipping before God, not in front of people.

2. **Prophets speak in front of people**

   The Greek word *pro* can describe a prophet's position *in front of people*. This lets us know a prophet's ministry is a public ministry.

3. **Prophets speak on behalf of the Lord**

   The Greek word *pro* can describe a prophet's responsibility to *"speak on behalf"* of the Lord. A prophet is an oracle of God, or the Lord's mouthpiece. He is only to speak on the Lord's behalf, not his own.

4. **Prophets speak in advance of something**

   The Greek word *pro* also carries with it the sense of a predictive ability and can be translated as one who *"speaks in advance."*

We know from Scripture that the church in Antioch had a large number of prophets that were flourishing. Acts 13:1 says, "prophets," plural, and so does Acts 11:27, which says, "And in these days came *prophets* from Jerusalem unto Antioch."

The Office of a 'Teacher'

Not only were there prophets in Antioch, but also a substantial group of *teachers*. Acts 13:1 says, "Now there were in the church that was at Antioch certain prophets and *teachers*...." The word "teachers" is a form of the Greek word *didaskalos*. In this verse, it is plural; and it describes *one who is a fabulous, masterful teacher.*

This word *didaskalos* is the Greek equivalent for the Hebrew word *rabbi*. It is used 47 times in the gospels, and it is derived from the word *didasko*, which means *to teach, to instruct, or to prescribe*. It primarily described *the relationship between a teacher and a pupil* or *between a master and an apprentice*. In a secular sense, it was used to describe *a theatrical dramatic teacher*. The word "teacher" is often translated "rabbi" or "master."

The teachers in the church at Antioch were *masterful, scriptural rabbis*, and like the prophets who were there, they too were thriving in their gift. Who were these teachers? We know from Acts 13:1 that Manaen and Saul (who is the apostle Paul) were both teachers. In First Timothy 2:7, Paul identifies himself as a "teacher of the Gentiles." We also know from Acts 18:24-26 that Aquila and his wife Priscilla, as well as Apollos, were also masterful teachers.

The Major Difference Between Prophets and Teachers

Now, you may be wondering who the prophets were in the church at Antioch. A careful reading of Acts 13:1 helps us determine who was who. The Bible says, "Now there were in the church that was at Antioch certain prophets and teachers; as Barnabas, and Simeon that was called Niger, and Lucius of Cyrene, and Manaen, which had been brought up with Herod the tetrarch, and Saul."

Notice the first three people mentioned: "...Barnabas, and Simeon that was called Niger, and Lucius of Cyrene...." History reveals that these three had no formal theological training. Therefore, they stood in the office of a prophet. A person doesn't have to be theologically trained to be a prophet. Prophets know the voice of the Holy Spirit and speak by revelation, or divine inspiration, and they usually speak spontaneously. Of course, it is always beneficial to have theological training when serving in any area of ministry. But these three particular men were not theologically trained, which lets us know they served in prophetic ministry.

The last two mentioned — Manaen and Saul — stood in the office of a teacher. These men were highly educated. Manaen had been brought up with Herod the tetrarch, another highly educated man. And Saul had undergone so much theological training he had been both a rabbi and a Pharisee. As teachers, these men needed more than spontaneity and inspiration. They needed to have a library of knowledge in their heads that they could access and use to instruct others. Although they did speak under the inspiration of the Holy Spirit, the expanse of scriptural knowledge they possessed was what the Spirit drew from as they stood in the position of teacher.

Again, the unlikely team that the Holy Spirit assembled to serve in the church at Antioch were "...Barnabas, and Simeon that was called Niger, and Lucius of Cyrene, and Manaen, which had been brought up with Herod the tetrarch, and Saul" (Acts 13:1). In our next lesson, we're going to see that only God could bring together such a culturally diverse group. But that is exactly what we find in Christ: all cultural and gender distinctions disappear. Differences such as skin color and ethnicity evaporate in Christ. This is a picture of the "new man" God was creating in the city of Antioch, and it was imperative for Paul to be there at that pivotal time.

Think about it. If Barnabas had brought Paul to Jerusalem, Paul would have been around people who looked like him, thought like him, and taught like him. The experience would have been extremely limited. But by bringing Paul to Antioch, he was able to rub elbows with people he would have never connected with in Jerusalem. He learned firsthand that in Christ, all cultural distinctions disappear and it prepared him for his apostolic ministry to the Gentiles. This demonstrates the importance of being in the right place at the right time.

STUDY QUESTIONS

**Study to shew thyself approved unto God, a workman that needeth
not to be ashamed, rightly dividing the word of truth.**
— 2 Timothy 2:15

1. In the church at Antioch, the gifts of the prophet and teacher were
    flourishing. In your own words, briefly describe the difference between
    these two vital ministry gifts. What must a teacher have to function
    that is not a requirement for a prophet? Who do you know in your
    church that functions in these gifts?

2. The group of leaders God assembled in Antioch was extremely
    diverse. Yet in His eyes, they were equal. Take a few moments to
    reflect on Acts 10:34,35; Romans 2:11 and 10:12; Galatians 2:6; and
    Ephesians 6:9. What character qualities of God are recurring in these
    verses? What does this say to you personally about the way you see
    and treat others?

PRACTICAL APPLICATION

But be ye doers of the word, and not hearers only,
deceiving your own selves.
— James 1:22

The Bible tells us that Barnabas was extremely instrumental in Paul's life.
He vouched for Paul's character and helped him connect with the apostles
in Jerusalem (*see* Acts 9:26-28). Then he went out and searched for Paul
and brought him to Antioch where they served together in ministry for
many years (*see* Acts 11:25,26).

1. Who has God placed in your life through the years that has been
    instrumental in your Christian development?

2. Share an example of how they have helped you reconnect with Jesus
    or remain in fellowship with His Church.

3. Who have you been able to help in their Christian walk? How have
    you been able to help them?

4. Is there anyone the Holy Spirit is bringing to mind that you could
    take the initiative to help right now?

TOPIC

The Right Place at the Right Time

SCRIPTURES

1. **Acts 13:1** — Now there were in the church that was at Antioch certain prophets and teachers; as Barnabas, and Simeon that was called Niger, and Lucius of Cyrene, and Manaen, which had been brought up with Herod the tetrarch, and Saul.

2. **Galatians 3:28** — There is neither Jew nor Greek, there is neither bond nor free, there is neither male nor female: for ye are all one in Christ Jesus.

3. **Colossians 3:11** — Where there is neither Greek nor Jew, circumcision nor uncircumcision, Barbarian, Scythian, bond nor free: but Christ is all, and in all.

GREEK WORDS

1. "there were" — ἦσαν (*esan*): there existed
2. "now" — δὲ (*de*): an exclamatory statement
3. "in" — κατά (*kata*): carries the sense of domination
4. "certain" — οὖσαν (*ousan*): a form of εἰμί (*eimi*); here, existing; having life and flourishing

SYNOPSIS

As we have seen in our previous two lessons, God was doing an incredible, unprecedented work in the city of Antioch. As early as 37 or 38 AD, a church was founded in this thriving metropolis, and its members were meeting in a cave that was located in a graveyard. It was from this very church that the apostle Paul and Barnabas were officially selected by the Holy Spirit and sent out on their first missionary journey.

After traveling many miles with stopovers in many cities — including Salamis, Iconium, Lystra, and Derbe — Paul and Barnabas returned to their home base in Antioch. The Bible says, "And when they were come, and had gathered the church together, they rehearsed all that God had done with them, and how he had opened the door of faith unto the Gentiles. And there they abode long time with the disciples" (Acts 14:27,28).

For Paul, Antioch was home, and he loved it. God had moved him there, and it was where he was equipped and trained for apostolic ministry. It was the right place and the right time for him to be there, and when you're in the right place at the right time, things really begin to come together like never before.

The emphasis of this lesson:

By directing Paul to Antioch, the Holy Spirit placed him in a multiracial environment where he could learn to serve side by side with Gentiles and Jews alike. He learned firsthand that in Christ, all cultural distinctions disappear, and it prepared him for his apostolic ministry to the Gentiles. Antioch was the right place for Paul to be, and it was the right time for him to be there.

A Brief Review of Our Anchor Verse

Looking again at our anchor verse in Acts 13:1, it says, "Now there were in the church that was at Antioch certain prophets and teachers; as Barnabas, and Simeon that was called Niger, and Lucius of Cyrene, and Manaen, which had been brought up with Herod the tetrarch, and Saul."

We have seen that the word "now," is the Greek word *de*, which in this verse is like *an exclamation mark*. It is the equivalent of the Holy Spirit excitedly saying, "Wow! Can you believe what was taking place in the church at Antioch? It's amazing!"

The Bible then says, "…There were in…." The phrase "there were" is the Greek word *esan*, which means *there existed* or *flourishing there*. And the word "in" is the Greek word *kata*, which always carries the idea of *domination*. The use of these words — "Now there were in" — tells us that the fivefold ministry gifts were *flourishing* and *dominating* the church at Antioch. With the ministries of apostles, prophets, evangelists, pastors, and teachers thriving, it is no wonder that Antioch became known as the "cradle of Christianity."

Antioch, Not Jerusalem,
Was the *Right Place* and *Right Time* for Paul

It is important to reiterate the fact that when Saul was saved, the Holy Spirit led him to Antioch, not Jerusalem. It would have been natural for him to gravitate toward Jerusalem because it was predominantly a Jewish setting. He had been trained as a Jewish Rabbi, he understood all the Jewish customs and traditions, and he spoke fluent Hebrew. But the Holy Spirit didn't lead Paul to Jerusalem; He led him to Antioch, because Antioch was the best place for him to receive the training he would need for his future.

It is interesting to note that after Acts Chapter 8, the city of Jerusalem rarely appears again in the book of Acts. When it does appear, it is usually not in a positive light. Even though the city of Jerusalem was and is very dear to the heart of God, it appears that the new work the Holy Spirit was doing in building the Church eventually shifted from Jerusalem to Antioch. That is a distance of 445 miles north, and during the First Century, that was a massive measure of space. Nevertheless, Antioch became the new hub where many wonderful things were happening and God was imparting new spiritual vision to believers.

For Saul of Tarsus, who became the apostle Paul, Antioch was home. In fact, throughout all of his early apostolic journeys, Antioch served as his base of operations. When he returned from his mission trips, he reported to the church in Antioch, not the church in Jerusalem. In Jerusalem, the believers were hung up on, weighed down, and distracted by their past religious upbringing. Even though they had come to faith in Christ, most believers in Jerusalem were tending toward Judaica thoughts, trying to be Jewish believers.

Not so in Antioch. They didn't have past religious hang-ups, and the majority of the congregation knew very little — if anything — about Jewish customs, rites, or rituals. They were free from the chains of religious traditions. In Antioch, God was creating what the apostle Paul called "the new man." In many ways, the church in Antioch was like a chalkboard that had never been written on. You might say it was a *new wineskin* that God was filling with the fresh wine of His Spirit. The people in Antioch were flexible in God's hands and receptive to the new things He was doing. He was creating something that could have never been created in the city of Jerusalem.

A Picture of 'The New Man'

It was into the ripe environment of Antioch that God placed Paul. Being surrounded by open-minded believers during this critical stage of his spiritual development taught Paul how to flow freely with the Holy Spirit. It also equipped him for apostolic ministry to the Gentile world. If Paul had gone to Jerusalem, his spiritual growth would have more than likely been stifled by the narrow-minded, religious thinking that had taken root in the people there. In Antioch, Paul was free to develop his teaching gift in a supportive, non-threatening environment and understand what the Church of the Lord Jesus Christ should look like.

In Antioch, Paul received a clear picture of "the new man" — or Church — and he described it in his letters to the churches. In Galatians 3:28, he said, "There is neither Jew nor Greek, there is neither bond nor free, there is neither male nor female: for ye are all one in Christ Jesus." And in Colossians 3:11, he added to this saying, "Where there is neither Greek nor Jew, circumcision nor uncircumcision, Barbarian, Scythian, bond nor free: but Christ is all, and in all."

Paul would have never received this revelation of the Church in Jerusalem, because in Jerusalem, there were no Barbarians, Scythians, or slaves. Virtually everyone in the church was of Jewish heritage. In Antioch, Paul learned to worship and serve side by side with people from many types of cultural distinctions, skin colors, and economic and educational backgrounds. God was — and still is — interested in restoring His relationship with every blend of human being. This made the emerging church at Antioch the right place and the right time for Paul's development.

The Great Diversity of the Leaders in Antioch

One of the main factors that made the church of Antioch such a great environment was the diversity of its spiritual leadership. We can see a picture of this diversity in Acts 13:1, which says, "Now there were in the church that was at Antioch certain prophets and teachers; as Barnabas, and Simeon that was called Niger, and Lucius of Cyrene, and Manaen, which had been brought up with Herod the tetrarch, and Saul."

In this verse, five leaders are mentioned: Barnabas, Simeon, Lucius, Manaen, and Saul. Only two of these men had a Hebrew background

— Saul and Barnabas. The other three — Simeon, Lucius, and Manaen — were Gentiles that had come to faith in Christ. This was a complete break from past tradition. For the first time, Jews and Gentiles were intermingled in a congregation, serving the Lord together as equal partners in the Body of Christ.

Although the information about these men in Acts 13:1 is limited, some knowledge about their lives can be gleaned. Here is some of what we know:

Barnabas was a Levite from the Gentile country of Cyprus, which was a region in Greece (*see* Acts 4:36). He was a distant Jew descended from the tribe of Levi, and because he was raised so far from Jerusalem, it is likely that he didn't grow up around the strict religious environment that was so characteristic of that city. Hence, he probably did not receive theological training.

Simeon is referred to in Scripture as "Niger," which is the Latin word meaning *black*. Scholars speculate that this indicates Simeon was probably a black man from Africa and may have even been the slave of a Roman family. Simeon served in a position of authority in the church of Antioch.

Lucius of Cyrene was from the region of Cyrene in northern Africa. Some scholars argue that Lucius was a man of North African heritage. The name "Lucius" actually means *light* or *bright*, which some suggest means he was perhaps a black man with light colored skin. Like Simeon, it seems he had come to Antioch from Africa and became a leader in the church.

Manaen was "brought up with Herod the tetrarch" and was, in fact, probably a relative of the family of Herod. The phrase "brought up" in this verse carries the idea of *being nourished by* the family of Herod. Because Manaen was Roman and likely descended from the royal family, he had received a Roman education. This is especially significant because educated Romans were raised to look down on foreigners as being uncouth barbarians who were classed as "less" than Romans. Manaen's position, alongside other ethnicities and skin colors, lets us know that he had broken free from the prejudices of his upbringing to work alongside two Africans and two Jews who were brothers in the Lord.

Paul, who was first called Saul, is the last leader of this supernatural gathering in the church in Antioch mentioned. Saul was born into a very well-connected, tremendously wealthy Jewish family who were also

Roman citizens. Being raised in a wealthy home, Saul was afforded the best education that money could buy. His hometown of Tarsus was a university city. He had also been theologically trained for his former positions as a rabbi and Pharisee. Consequently, Saul was the most religiously instructed and possessed the greatest breadth of scriptural knowledge of any of his peers among the Antioch church leadership.

To assemble this particular group in the First Century broke all norms of society — it was truly a supernatural situation that only God could arrange. It was unthinkable for these men with their extremely diverse backgrounds and cultures to sit together at the same table, much less serve together as equal leaders. Think about it: we have an unorthodox, displaced Jew (Barnabas); a black man from Africa who was possibly a former slave (Simeon); a fair-skinned black man from northern Africa (Lucius of Cyrene); a highly educated man of royalty who grew up with Herod (Manaen); and a highly educated former rabbi and Pharisee (Paul). This is a partnership between nobility and slaves, wealthy and poor, educated and uneducated, black and white, Jew and Gentile. This arrangement was revolutionary and would have never taken place in the church in Jerusalem.

By directing Paul to Antioch, the Holy Spirit placed him in a multiracial environment where he could learn to serve side by side with Gentiles and Jews alike. Although Jerusalem was a fine place, it was confining and lacked the essential ingredients Paul needed to be properly trained for his purpose as an apostle to the Gentiles. Indeed, when you're in the right place at the right time, God surrounds you with the people and circumstances that duly prepare you for your future. In our next lesson, we will identify what the right balance is for a powerful environment.

STUDY QUESTIONS

Study to shew thyself approved unto God, a workman that needeth not to be ashamed, rightly dividing the word of truth.
— 2 Timothy 2:15

1. Without question, the diversity of the leaders at the church in Antioch was vast. What new fascinating facts did you learn about these leaders? What detail was most surprising to you? What aspects of this leadership team clearly confirm that only God could have orchestrated it?

2. Paul loved Antioch. It was the place God had brought him, and it became his home base. Do you have a place you call your spiritual home — a church where you're being trained with people who are sharpening you (*see* Proverbs 27:17)? If so, take a moment and describe your church and share what you most appreciate about it.

3. Like Paul, when you're following the leading of the Holy Spirit, He will bring you to the right place at the right time. According to Colossians 3:15, what is one of the most important internal signs that God is leading you to do something or go somewhere? If He is *not* leading you, what will you lack? (Also consider Isaiah 55:12.) What do you sense the Holy Spirit is leading you to do in your current season?

PRACTICAL APPLICATION

**But be ye doers of the word, and not hearers only,
deceiving your own selves.
—James 1:22**

1. Imagine God is sending you back in time to the church in Jerusalem in the First Century. His assignment for you is to speak words of wisdom — and warning — to believers in that church who are judging whether or not what is happening at the church in Antioch is truly of God. Given the insight you have, what would you tell these believers?

2. Antioch was the right place for Paul to be trained and prepared for his apostolic ministry to the Gentiles. God placed him there at just the right time. How about you? Have you moved away from — or not gone to — the place God directed you to go? Are you where you need to be in order to receive the training to fulfill God's purpose on your life?

3. When you look back over the places (and situations) you have experienced, in what specific ways can you see that God has prepared and equipped you for where you are now and for where He is taking you? What can you do differently to better cooperate with the work of the Holy Spirit in your life?

TOPIC

The Right Balance
for a Powerful Environment

SCRIPTURES

1. **Acts 13:1** — Now there were in the church that was at Antioch certain prophets and teachers; as Barnabas, and Simeon that was called Niger, and Lucius of Cyrene, and Manaen, which had been brought up with Herod the tetrarch, and Saul.

2. **Proverbs 27:17** (*NLT*) — As iron sharpens iron, so a friend sharpens a friend.

3. **Galatians 3:26-28** (*NLT*) — For you are all children of God through faith in Christ Jesus. And all who have been united with Christ in baptism have put on Christ, like putting on new clothes. There is no longer Jew or Gentile, slave or free, male and female. For you are all one in Christ Jesus.

4. **Proverbs 20:24** (*AMPC*) — Man's steps are ordered by the Lord. How then can a man understand his way?

GREEK WORDS

1. "there were" — ἦσαν (*esan*): there existed

2. "now" — δὲ (*de*): an exclamatory statement

3. "in" — κατά (*kata*): carries the sense of domination

SYNOPSIS

If you were to travel to the region of southern Turkey today, you would find the ruins of the ancient city of Antioch, including a cave where the believers in Antioch first met. From this thriving church, Paul and Barnabas learned how to be spiritual leaders and were sent out on their first missionary journey.

Surprisingly, it was in this same location that Paul and Barnabas came to a major disagreement regarding who to take with them on their second missions trip. Barnabas wanted to take his nephew John Mark, but Paul didn't because John Mark had abandoned them when they were in the city of Pamphylia. Acts 15:39 says, "And the contention was so sharp between them, that they departed asunder one from the other...."

As tragic as this rift may seem, God used the situation to create two ministry teams that went out in two different directions. As a result, more lives were touched and saved by the Gospel than any one team could have accomplished alone. Indeed, God will make "...all things work together for good to those who love God, to those who are called according to His purpose" (Romans 8:28 *NKJV*).

The emphasis of this lesson:

Having a balance of new and older leaders is very important when it comes to having a powerful spiritual environment. They bring life, vitality, and stability to a church, making it feel as fresh and exciting as it is well-balanced and doctrinally sound. Antioch had the right balance of leaders for a powerful environment, and it was exactly where Paul needed to be.

A Review of Our Anchor Verse

In Acts 13:1, the Bible says, "Now there were in the church that was at Antioch certain prophets and teachers; as Barnabas, and Simeon that was called Niger, and Lucius of Cyrene, and Manaen, which had been brought up with Herod the tetrarch, and Saul."

We have seen that the word "now," which is the Greek word *de*, is used here as *an exclamatory statement*. It is like the Holy Spirit is lifting His voice saying, "Wow! What was taking place in the church of Antioch was phenomenal!"

The verse goes on to say, "...There were in the church...." The phrase "there were" is the Greek word *esan*, which would better be translated *there existed*, and it carries the idea of *something flourishing*. Even the word "in" is important. It is the Greek word *kata*, which always carries the idea of *domination*. All these words taken together let us know that the fivefold ministry gifts were *thriving in* and *dominating* the church at Antioch — especially the gifts of prophecy and teaching."

There are five primary leaders mentioned in Acts 13:1 — Saul, Barnabas, Simeon, Lucius, and Manaen. Only two of these men — Saul and Barnabas — had a Hebrew background. The other three — Simeon, Lucius, and Manaen — were Gentiles. This was a complete break from past tradition. For the first time, Jews and Gentiles were worshiping and serving the Lord together as equal partners in the Body of Christ.

A Snapshot of the Leaders at Antioch

Although the information about the five church leaders mentioned in Acts 13:1 is limited, some knowledge about their lives can be gleaned. Here is a recap of what we know:

Barnabas was a Levite from the Gentile country of Cyprus, which was a region in Greece (*see* Acts 4:36). He was a distant Jew descended from the tribe of Levi, and because he was raised so far from Jerusalem, it is likely that he didn't grow up around the strict religious environment that was so characteristic of that city. This means he probably did not receive theological training.

Simeon is referred to in Scripture as "Niger," which is the Latin word meaning *black*. Scholars speculate that this indicates Simeon was probably a black man from Africa and may have even been the slave of a Roman family. Yet, despite where he came from or who he was, he served in a position of authority in the church of Antioch.

Lucius of Cyrene was from the region of Cyrene in northern Africa. Some scholars argue that Lucius was a man of North African heritage. The name "Lucius" actually means *light* or *bright*, which some suggest indicates he was perhaps a black man with light colored skin. Yet, regardless of the identity of this man, it seems he had come to Antioch from Northern Africa and became a leader in the church.

Manaen was "brought up with Herod the tetrarch" and was, in fact, probably a relative of the family of Herod. In Greek, the phrase "brought up" carries the idea of *being nourished by*. Hence, the family of Herod probably took Manaen in as a member, which made him descended from the royal family and a Roman. This means he would have received a Roman education and would have been raised to look down on foreigners as being uncouth barbarians who were classed as "less" than Romans. Manaen's position at the church in Antioch, alongside other ethnicities and skin colors, lets us know that he had broken free from the prejudices of his upbringing to work alongside two Africans and two Jews who were brothers in the Lord.

Paul — who was still called Saul at that time — is the last leader of this supernatural gathering in the church in Antioch mentioned. Saul was born into a very well-connected, tremendously wealthy Jewish family who were also Roman citizens. Being raised in a wealthy home, Saul was afforded the best education that money could buy. His hometown of Tarsus was a university city. He had also been theologically trained for his former positions as a rabbi and Pharisee. Consequently, Saul was the most religiously instructed and possessed the greatest breadth of scriptural knowledge of any of his peers among the Antioch church leadership.

Stop and think about the extreme diverse backgrounds and cultures of these five leaders:

Barnabas: an unorthodox, displaced Jew

Simeon: a black man who was possibly a former slave

Lucius of Cyrene: a fair-skinned black man from northern Africa

Manaen: a highly educated man of royalty who grew up with Herod

Paul: a highly educated former rabbi and Pharisee

In the First Century, these cultures did not connect. For them to sit together at the same table was simply unheard of, much less serve together as equal leaders. Nonetheless, in Antioch, we see a partnership between nobility and slaves, wealthy and poor, educated and uneducated, black and white, Jew and Gentile. This arrangement was revolutionary and would have never taken place in the church in Jerusalem.

A Balance Between New and Old Leaders

There was quite a mix of personalities in the leaders at Antioch, and all of them brought something unique to the table. There were new believers and older believers; some had religious backgrounds, and others had little-to-no religious upbringing.

New leaders are often more open to new ideas and are flexible concerning a fresh move of God's Spirit. As such, they bring a much-needed vitality to the Body of Christ. *Older leaders*, on the other hand, bring rock-solid stability, experience, and a firmer understanding of the Word of God.

Having a balance of new and older leaders is very important when it comes to having a powerful environment.

If there are too many young leaders in a church, that congregation can become imbalanced, unstable, and immature because it lacks the solid foundation of Scripture. In contrast, too many older leaders can cause a church to become limited by a strict adherence to tradition and an unwillingness to change or try new things. This can greatly reduce the ability of the Holy Spirit to move as He pleases. Again, having the right mix of young and old leaders will bring life, vitality, and stability to a church, making it feel as fresh and exciting as it is well-balanced and doctrinally sound.

The church of Antioch was a diverse mixture of social class, education, and age. There were new and older, more seasoned believers. There were those who had had years of religious training and those who had no training at all until they came to Christ. Likewise, there were wealthy nobility, former slaves, and individuals with different skin colors all serving and worshiping together.

The Key Role Paul Played at Antioch

One of the players on the leadership team in Antioch was Saul of Tarsus — who we know became the apostle Paul. He provided the congregation of Antioch with a solid foundation of the Word of God. If someone taught something that was in error, Paul could quickly bring them back in line by having them reexamine what they were saying in light of the truth of Scripture.

His years of study and Jewish heritage provided him with a wealth of knowledge. Jesus' lineage, Messianic prophecies, and the Shekinah glory of God were easy topics for him to teach on since he had such a grasp of Old Testament Scriptures. As a trained rabbi and theologian, he was like a fish in water when it came to these significant topics. They represented his former identity and were his field of expertise.

Yes, Manaen had been brought up in the royal lineage of Herod and was highly educated, but he had not been raised in the Scriptures like Paul. Barnabas was a distant Jew from the tribe of Levi, but he grew up in Cyprus, which was nothing like the structured religious environment in which Paul grew up. Moreover, neither Simeon, who was probably a former slave, nor Lucius of Cyrene were afforded a higher education or theological training — nor were they Jews. Only Paul could succinctly fill this role.

It is not difficult to imagine how expounding on the Old Testament in a thorough and balanced manner would have quickly become Paul's niche within the church of Antioch. In many ways, Paul was like a living, breathing Hebrew concordance and Bible commentary. Having him on their teaching staff gave the believers in Antioch unprecedented access to an expert on Jewish culture and the Old Testament.

And because he was well versed in the Word of God, Paul was also able to discern what was doctrinally sound and what was contrary to the teaching of Scripture. This became extremely important as the church of Antioch began to move into realms of the Spirit that were new to them and to receive new revelation they had never heard before. Paul brought just the right balance to the environment to keep the church securely founded while growing in its spiritual capacity. Having this kind of balance created a powerful spiritual environment for tremendous growth.

As Paul Sharpened Others,
He Himself Was Radically Changed

As we've noted previously, God will use your environment — the people, places, and opportunities around you — to shape and sharpen your gifts. And while He is in the process of developing your gifts, He will simultaneously use you to sharpen the gifts in others. We find this principle in Proverbs 27:17 (*NLT*), which says, "As iron sharpens iron, so a friend sharpens a friend."

Through Paul's role as the "go-to" Bible teacher in the church of Antioch, he learned how to effectively communicate the connections between the Old and New Covenants. At the same time, living and ministering in Antioch's diverse environment was also strategic to his developing an understanding of God's vision of the Church and what it meant to be a *new man* in Christ (*see* 2 Corinthians 5:17).

In Antioch, blacks, whites, Jews, and Gentiles all mingled together in leadership and worship. This was something that had never existed before. God used the plethora of nationalities and cultures represented in the congregation to give Saul (Paul) a broad perspective of the Gospel and its mission and to paint a powerful picture of what the Church should look like — a colorful tapestry of people from all walks of life.

Through the death, burial, and resurrection of Jesus Christ, God was creating one *new man* — the Body of Christ. The wall separating Jews and Gentiles had been broken down and destroyed, and salvation was equally available to all of mankind. Saul lived and breathed this truth every day as he rubbed elbows with people from different cultures who were saved and filled with the Holy Ghost.

Just think of what a radical shift in thinking this was for him! Saul, a Hebrew of Hebrews, "circumcised on the eighth day," was worshiping and working side by side with uncircumcised people from different ethnic groups and backgrounds who had made Jesus Christ their Lord and Savior.

Saul saw with his own eyes the power of God working in and through people from all nations. How could he argue with a Greek being saved? How could he argue with an African being a leader in the church? All of this was happening right in front of him. People of diverse backgrounds were serving alongside Saul as elders in the church and functioning as prophets and teachers. It was a new revelation of the *new man* in Christ — not from one blood or one nation, but from *many*. This was a radical idea!

It was from this revelation that the apostle would later write...

> **For you are all children of God through faith in Christ Jesus. And all who have been united with Christ in baptism have put on Christ, like putting on new clothes. There is no longer Jew or Gentile, slave or free, male and female. For you are all one in Christ Jesus.**
>
> **Galatians 3:26-28 (*NLT*)**

If Paul had gone to Jerusalem, it is doubtful that he ever would have understood this truth the way he grasped it in Antioch. To be clear, Jerusalem was — and still is — very dear to God. But it was a city steeped in Jewish tradition. In fact, many of the converted Jewish leaders there were arguing and debating about how to take Gentile Christians and turn them into Jewish Christians. This environment would have stunted Paul's growth. He had to be placed in the environment at Antioch in order to be equipped and prepared.

So What Environment Are You In?

Are you where *God* placed you in the Body of Christ (*see* 1 Corinthians 12:18) — or are you just where *you* want to be? Maybe where you're located right now is your "Holy Spirit University" just as Antioch was for Paul.

It might be that God has asked you to go somewhere and you have struggled with it. You've asked, *Lord, why in the world would You take me there?* But never forget that the Bible teaches: "Man's steps are ordered by the Lord. How then can a man understand his way?" (Proverbs 20:24 *AMPC*). God ordered Saul's steps for him to be in the church at Antioch. It was not where he would have naturally gravitated, but it was where God knew he needed to be.

Friend, God knows what you need and is working a plan to fully develop the gifts He has placed in you. However, you have to allow Him to place you in the environment He knows is best. If you will humbly submit to where God wants you to be, He will fully prepare you for the next phase of your life.

STUDY QUESTIONS

**Study to shew thyself approved unto God, a workman that needeth
not to be ashamed, rightly dividing the word of truth.
— 2 Timothy 2:15**

1. In your own words, describe the benefits of having a balance of both *new* and *older* leaders in a church. What does each group uniquely bring to the table? Which group would you say you fall into?
2. In light of the civil unrest taking place in many of our cities, why do you think it is crucial for you and all of God's people to understand that His Church — the Body of Christ — is made up of blacks, whites, Hispanics, and all nationalities mingled together as one?
3. Through the apostle Paul, God said no one is "…to estimate and think of himself more highly than he ought [not to have an exaggerated opinion of his own importance]…" (Romans 12:3 *AMPC*). To understand how valuable this attitude of *humility* is in God's eyes, read what He said in these verses:
   • James 4:6; 1 Peter 5:5

- Proverbs 22:4; 29:23
- Matthew 18:4; James 4:10
- Philippians 2:4-9

PRACTICAL APPLICATION

> But be ye doers of the word, and not hearers only,
> deceiving your own selves.
> —James 1:22

1. Rick shared how he became the go-to guy for understanding the Greek meaning of New Testament words in the university church where he first served. It was — and still is — his niche in the Church. Do you know what *your* niche is? What unique gifting do you bring to the table at your church? (Very often it is what people often seek you out for help with.)

2. In Antioch, blacks, whites, Jews, and Gentiles all mingled together in leadership and worship. It was a powerful picture of what the Church should look like — a colorful tapestry of people from all walks of life. Be honest: Do you believe that salvation through Christ is available to *all* people of *all* nationalities and cultures? If not, why? Pray and ask God to help you see people the way He sees them.

3. Are you in a church environment where your gifts are being developed? Who are you in relationship with who is sharpening you, and in what ways are you being sharpened (spiritually stretched and developed)?

LESSON 5

TOPIC

Are You in the Right Place for God To Develop You?

SCRIPTURES

1. **Acts 13:1,2** — Now there were in the church that was at Antioch certain prophets and teachers; as Barnabas, and Simeon that was called

Niger, and Lucius of Cyrene, and Manaen, which had been brought up with Herod the tetrarch, and Saul. As they ministered to the Lord, and fasted, the Holy Ghost said, Separate me Barnabas and Saul for the work whereunto I have called them.

GREEK WORDS

1. "ministered" — λειτουργέω (*leitourgeo*): one who served the state as a full-time employee; one who serves full-time in public religious service; used in the Old Testament Septuagint to depict the service of priests and Levites

2. "Lord" — κύριος (*kurios*): lord, or supreme master

3. "fasted" — νηστεύω (*nesteuo*): to abstain from food; to fast for a dedicated time for prayer or direction

4. "said" — εἶπεν (*eipen*): literally, said; this means the Holy Spirit's voice can be distinctly heard

5. "separate" — ἀφορίζω (*aphoridzo*): to mark off, to set boundaries around; to specifically set aside; to dedicate for a special purpose; to designate

6. "now" — δὲ (*de*): an exclamatory statement

7. "for" — εἰς (*eis*): literally, into; denotes movement, purpose, even transition

8. "work" — ἔργον (*ergon*): an action, deed, or activity; referred to a person's occupation, one's labor, or things produced by someone's effort or life; a person's line of work, his career, his occupation, his labor, or his profession

9. "called" — προσκαλέω (*proskaleo*): a compound of πρός (*pros*) and καλέω (*kaleo*); the word πρός (*pros*) means toward and indicates a close encounter; the word καλέω (*kaleo*) means to beckon, call, or summon for a specific purpose; personally summoned for a specific purpose

SYNOPSIS

For nearly 2,000 years, the cave located in the necropolis of Antioch has been recognized as the location where the church of Antioch began — the place where Jesus' disciples were first called Christians. When this church first started, there was no persecution from the government. This allowed the church to grow and become a very strong, thriving spiritual family.

Yet even in the midst of unhindered prosperity, the church at Antioch faced challenges from time to time. Acts 15:1 records one of these situations saying, "And certain men which came down from Judea taught the brethren, and said, Except ye be circumcised after the manner of Moses, ye cannot be saved." Immediately, Paul and Barnabas sharply disagreed with this teaching and took a stand to defend the truth — that we are saved *by grace, through faith* (*see* Ephesians 2:1-9).

Indeed, conflicts will arise — even when you're in the right place at the right time. Paul could attest to that fact. Yet, he never let any of those trying events move him from where he knew he was supposed to be, and neither should you.

The emphasis of this lesson:

Being in the right place at the right time is vital for you to be prepared for God's call on your life. By serving in full-time ministry at Antioch, Saul was equipped to be launched into his calling. Likewise, if you stay where you are supposed to be, it will lead you to God's destination for your life.

A Real-Life Example
From the Pages of Rick's Life

From the moment you surrender your life to Christ and make Him your Lord and Savior, He begins to direct your steps. The Bible says, "The steps of a [good] man are directed and established by the Lord when He delights in his way [and He busies Himself with his every step]" (Psalm 37:23 *AMPC*).

Rick Renner can personally testify that this is true. When he was finishing high school and making plans for college, his choice was Oral Roberts University, but God had another place in mind. He redirected Rick to a secular university, and it proved to be the perfect place for him to be trained in learning how to read the Greek New Testament, develop the skill of writing, and understand the ins and outs of the publishing world.

Additionally, it was during that same season that God placed him in a university church filled with young believers and a few older believers. There he learned how to minister and flow in the Holy Spirit. Likewise, he became skilled at interpreting and expounding from the Greek New

Testament. These formative college years prepared Rick for the next place God directed him, which was Fort Smith, Arkansas.

In Arkansas, Rick attended and served at a very large Baptist church where Dr. Bill Bennett was pastor. Dr. Bennett was a brilliant theologian who understood and presented the Greek New Testament in extraordinary ways. Like a caring spiritual father, Dr. Bennett took Rick under his wing and taught him how to accurately assimilate the original Greek text with New Testament doctrine. He also helped Rick develop the discipline and dedication he would need to advance to the next place God was bringing him and his wife Denise.

After completing his assignment in Arkansas, Rick and Denise began an extensive traveling ministry, taking his unique style of biblical teaching all across the United States. Each year he spoke hundreds of times in numerous churches, all the while cultivating close friendships with pastors and their congregations. Little did he know that these relationships would become his financial lifeline when he and Denise accepted their next assignment in the former Soviet Union.

If Rick had skipped any of these phases — or left one of these God-ordained places prematurely — he would have missed developing something that was vital for him to have where he is now. His life is a demonstration of how being in the right place at the right time is vital to the preparation and the ultimate execution of the call of God on your life.

The Five Leaders at Antioch 'Ministered to the Lord and Fasted'

When Barnabas went to Tarsus and found Saul and brought him back to Antioch, Saul was in the right place at the right time. It was the perfect environment for him to hone his gifts and be molded into the man he needed to be to fulfill his God-ordained purpose as an apostle to the Gentiles.

Looking once more at our anchor verse in Acts 13:1, it says, "Now there were in the church that was at Antioch certain prophets and teachers; as Barnabas, and Simeon that was called Niger, and Lucius of Cyrene, and Manaen, which had been brought up with Herod the tetrarch, and Saul." We have seen in the past two lessons that this group of leaders was made up of quite a mix of cultures, skin colors, and class distinctions. God was creating a vivid picture of the Church, the *new man*, and it was a tapestry of people from all walks of life that had never been assembled before. (For more details on this concept of the *new man*, please review Lessons 3 and 4.)

Then when we come to Acts 13:2, the Bible reveals what these leaders were doing together. Scripture says, "As they ministered to the Lord, and fasted, the Holy Ghost said, Separate me Barnabas and Saul for the work whereunto I have called them." Let's unpack some of the key words in this passage, starting with the word "ministered."

In Greek, the word "ministered" is *leitourgeo*, and it was used to describe *one who served the state as a full-time employee* or *one who serves full-time in public religious service*. It is used in the Old Testament Septuagint to depict *the service of priests and Levites*. The use of this word *leitourgeo* tells us that at this early moment in the history of the Church, there were people in full-time ministry. All five of these church leaders in Antioch had dedicated their lives to serving the Lord.

The word "Lord" is the Greek word *kurios*, and it means *lord*, or *supreme master*. This indicates that these leaders looked to the Lord as the supreme voice of authority in their lives. Furthermore, the Scripture says they "fasted," which is the Greek word *nesteuo*, and it means *to abstain from food*; *to fast for a dedicated time or purpose in prayer*. They were really seeking God's direction for the next phase of their ministry.

The Holy Spirit Said, 'Separate Me Barnabas and Saul'

As the leaders in Antioch fasted, "…the Holy Ghost said, Separate me Barnabas and Saul for the work whereunto I have called them" (Acts 13:2). In Greek, the word "said" is *eipen*, which literally means *said*. This indicates that *the Holy Spirit's voice can be distinctly heard*. We know from our previous study that Barnabas, Simeon, and Lucius were all prophets, so it is likely that this prophetic word came through one of them. When they heard this instruction, they knew it was the voice of the Holy Spirit.

And the Spirit said, "…Separate me Barnabas and Saul…." The word "separate" is the Greek word *aphoridzo*, which means *to mark off*, or *to set boundaries around*. It can also mean *to specifically set aside*; *to dedicate for a special purpose*; or *to designate*. What's interesting is that while it doesn't appear in the King James Version, in the original Greek, the word *de*

— which we saw in Acts 13:1 — appears in this verse. It could be translated as the word "now," and it is like *an exclamation mark*, communicating *urgency* and *immediacy*.

So when the Holy Spirit said, "…Separate me Barnabas and Saul…," He was literally saying, "Mark these two men off and set boundaries around them; set them aside and dedicate them for My special purpose." At that point, Barnabas and Saul had passed the test and were prepared to launch out into the assignment God had for them.

Saul and Barnabas
Were 'Called' to Do a Specific 'Work'

The Bible says these men were to be designated "…for the work whereunto I have called them" (Acts 13:2). The word "for" in Greek is the word *eis*, which literally means *into*. It denotes *movement, purpose, even transition*. The use of this word indicates that sometimes there is a period of time that is needed for us to move or transition to get from where we are to where we need to be.

This brings us to the word "work," which is a translation of the Greek word *ergon*. It describes *an action, deed, or activity and often referred to a person's occupation, one's labor, or things produced by someone's effort or life*. This word *ergon* can also refer to *a person's line of work, his career, his occupation, his labor, or his profession; it denoted the result of hard work or hard labor*. This word is so all-encompassing that it pictures *actions, beliefs, and conduct*.

Finally, we have the word "called" — a translation of the Greek word *proskaleo*, which is a compound of the words *pros* and *kaleo*. The word *pros* means *toward* and indicates *a close encounter;* the word *kaleo* means *to beckon, call, or summon for a specific purpose*. When *pros* and *kaleo* are compounded to form *proskaleo*, it means *personally summoned for a specific purpose*.

Just as God had a very specific calling for Barnabas and Saul, He has a specific calling for you. You are not an accident or a mistake. You were brought into this world for a specific purpose, and it is God's intention for you to fulfill it. When you get into the right place at the right time, you will clearly hear the Holy Spirit speak to you, just as He spoke to Saul and Barnabas.

'Saul' Became 'Paul' and Was Launched Into Ministry

With this one directive from the Holy Spirit, Saul was launched into his calling. The year was approximately 45 AD — about eight years after he'd had an encounter with the Lord on the road to Damascus and several years since he had first arrived in Antioch. He had been called and given his assignment from the beginning (*see* Acts 9:15), but he was not ready to step into it until that moment.

After proving himself faithful during those years of preparation in Antioch, Saul had arrived at the golden moment for his dream to be birthed. With this clear word from Heaven, the leaders in Antioch laid hands on Saul, and he stepped out in faith to begin his apostolic ministry with Barnabas at his side.

From that moment on, Scripture indicates that Saul was called Paul (*see* Acts 13:9), and he launched out into his apostolic ministry to the Gentile world. The trail of God's will led Paul to places he would never naturally gravitate to — specifically Antioch. If Paul would have chosen where he would serve after he was saved, it would have likely been the church at Jerusalem. But the church in Jerusalem would have never prepared Paul for his ministry to the Gentiles.

By going to and staying in Antioch, Paul rubbed shoulders and worked hand-in-hand with Gentiles and Jews every day. The congregation was made up of former slaves, nobility, the educated, the uneducated, and people of multiple languages and skin colors. God gave him an up-close view of what He wants His Church to look like. Antioch was the right place and the right time to train Paul for his future.

What Does All This Mean to You?

As we wrap up this final lesson, you need to stop and make an honest evaluation of where you are:

Have you allowed God to place you in the right environment to equip and prepare you for His plan? If the answer is yes, are you doing everything the Holy Spirit has prompted you to do within that right environment to prepare for your divine assignment?

Being prepared is a vital part of doing God's will. It's a part you cannot rush or skip over. The bigger His plan, the more preparation and equipping you need. If you stay where you're supposed to be in that place of preparation, God will begin to refine His purpose and call for your life. It will begin to make sense to your head and your heart, and God's ways will become clearer.

Sometimes in this process, you may accidentally detour from what God intended for you. If you make that mistake — if the will of God points one way and you've gone a different way — repent. Go back to the last thing He told you and get back on track. Make things right with God, within you, and with others. You must not deviate from God's appointed place and time for you.

Friend, set aside time to get quiet on the inside, and let the Holy Spirit show you where you need to be sharpened and developed. Be willing to hear whatever God wants to say to you. Determine to set aside your own plans and get into alignment with God's plan — *whatever* it is and *wherever* it is!

STUDY QUESTIONS

Study to shew thyself approved unto God, a workman that needeth not to be ashamed, rightly dividing the word of truth.
— 2 Timothy 2:15

1. Do you wonder if you can hear the voice of God and receive answers for your life? The answer is, *Yes you can!* Although you may not hear Him speak audibly, He is communicating with you on a regular basis. To understand some of the ways God speaks to you and what your part is in hearing Him, consider these verses:
   - Jeremiah 33:3; 29:12,13; Psalm 91:14,15; James 1:5
   - Psalm 25:9,12; 32:8; 73:24; Isaiah 30:21
   - John 14:26; 16:13
   - 2 Timothy 3:16,17; Psalm 19:7-11; 119:105; Proverbs 2:1-12

2. Oftentimes, we tend to worry and then get in a hurry because things are not moving as fast as we would like. To help you slow down and get God's perspective, take time to meditate on these important truths.

- Ecclesiastes 3:11
- Isaiah 55:8,9
- Psalm 46:10
- 1 Peter 5:6

PRACTICAL APPLICATION

**But be ye doers of the word, and not hearers only,
deceiving your own selves.
—James 1:22**

1. Rick shared how each place God had brought him was essential to developing what he needed for the next place. How about you? When you look back over your life, what are some of the specific phases or seasons that God has brought you through? Have you skipped going somewhere God wanted you to be — or left prematurely? If so, from where did you leave?

2. If Paul would have chosen where he wanted to serve after he was saved, he would have likely chosen the church at Jerusalem, but it would have never prepared him for his calling. Antioch was where he needed to be. What place (or places) did God choose for you to be that you would have never chosen to go? What helps you see that it was the right place at the right time for you?

3. Be honest: Have you allowed God to place you in the right environment to equip and prepare you for *His plan*? If the answer is yes, are you doing everything the Holy Spirit has prompted you to do within that right environment to prepare for your divine assignment? If not, what do you need His strength to help you accomplish?

4. Have you accidentally detoured from what God intended for you? If you've made the mistake of doing something different than what He told you, repent. Go back to the last thing He told you to do and do it. Make things right with God, within you, and with others. Today is a great day to make a fresh start in obeying what God told you to do!

Notes

Notes

www.ingramcontent.com/pod-product-compliance
Lightning Source LLC
Chambersburg PA
CBHW071747020426
42331CB00008B/2208